A Little Book
of St Patrick

Compiled and introduced by
Don Mullan

First published in 2004 by
a little book company
12466 Senda Road, San Diego, CA 92128, USA
and
11 Hillsbrook Crescent, Dublin 12, Ireland
E mail: alittlebookcompany@eircom.net
Web site: www.alittlebookcompany.com

ISBN 0-9547047-0-3

To
Bishop Patrick Ahern
New York
and his gracious secretary
Peggy Peet

and to John McCarthy and
The Friendly Sons of St Patrick
of Westchester Country

for all their wonderful friendship
and support

Acknowledgements

The publisher and editor gratefully acknowledge the permission of the following to quote from material in their copyright: *Patrick in his own words,* copyright © Joseph Duffy 2000. Published by Veritas Publications, 7-8 Lower Abbey Street, Dublin 1, Ireland.

Author's Acknowledgements

Sincere thanks are owed to the following for their kind support and assistance with this publication:

First and foremost to Seán O Boyle of Columba Press who by suggesting I do this little book on Ireland's patron saint, introduced me to his writings which, I must confess, I had never read before. I was deeply moved by the discovery of the real Patrick and not the one of myths and legends. I am also grateful to Bishop Joseph Duffy whose book, *Patrick in his own words* was the primary source of this little book. Readers are encouraged to deepen their knowledge of Patrick by ordering Dr Duffy's

book from Veritas Publications, 7-8 Lower
Abbey Street, Dublin 1, Ireland. ISBN: 1-
85390-525-9.
I also wish to thank Gary Burke, RIP, who
departed this life on 7 March 2003, for his
interest and encouragement of my work. Also
the staff of Columba Press; Sr Madonna and
Sr Donna and the staff of Pauline Books and
Media, Boston, USA; Seamus Cashman who
planted the seed of this Little Book series; and
last but not least, my family: Margaret,
Thérèse, Carl and Emma for their continued
kindness and warmth.

We sometimes forget that Jesus was Jewish – not Christian. In the same way, we often forget that St Patrick was British, not Irish. Indeed, it can be argued, he was Britain's greatest gift to Ireland long before its colonisation. A rediscovery of Patrick, by both the Irish and British, might help to underpin our promising, though fraught, Peace Process.

Patrick's love of Ireland and the Irish is all the more amazing when we consider his first introduction was as a slave boy. In adolescence he was plucked from a privileged position by marauding Irish bandits. His father, Calpornius, was a collector of imperial Roman taxes and a member of the local ruling council. The location of their Roman settlement is not definitively known, but some scholars believe it was close to the mouth of the river Severn, Wales.

After his escape from his Irish slave master and return home, Patrick travelled to Gaul in France to commence his studies for the priesthood. We do not have definitive dates for his birth and death. We have approximate dates for his return to Ireland as a missionary, c. 461, and his death c. 493.

This little book of St Patrick is based on two documents written by Patrick: *Confession* and *Letter to the Soldiers of Coroticus*. Both contain autobiographical details and they reveal a man of extraordinary biblical faith, prayer, courage, determination and loyalty, especially to his Irish converts.

While relatively short documents, the *Confession* and *Letter* reveal a very human man who struggled with self-doubt, loneliness, ridicule and abuse. He suffered the betrayal of a lifelong friend and the resulting humiliation of a public investigation. He experienced homesickness for both his family in Britain and his religious brothers in Gaul. Through it all, one sees his growing love of the Irish, founded on his love of Christ. This, indeed, culminates in his fearless defence of, and identification with, the Irish in his condemnation of the brutal racism of Coroticus and his men. He writes: 'They think it a matter of contempt that we are Irish.'

The final quotes in this little book are taken from near the beginning of Patrick's *Confession*.

They are his creed and reveal his deep faith, drawn from the endless well of God's love revealed in the Father, Son and Holy Spirit. While there is no mention of shamrocks, tradition says that Patrick's used it to teach the doctrine of the Trinity. Patrick's faith in the Holy Trinity was the powerhouse that drove him to risk his life for the Irish who, in the 5th century, were considered to live at 'the very ends of the earth'.

Tradition says he is buried at Downpatrick, Co Down, Ireland, alongside St Brigid and St Colmcille. His feast day is March 17.

Don Mullan
Dublin
17 March 2004

The Writings of St Patrick

Confession

I am Patrick, a sinner,
the most rustic and least of all the faithful
… My father Calpornius, a deacon…
came from the village
of Bannaventaberniae.
It was there that I was taken captive.

I was taken into captivity to Ireland
with many thousands of people.
This is where I am now.
I was an adolescent,
almost a speechless boy,
and I did not know the true God.

[In Ireland]
the Lord made me aware
of my unbelief
that I migh … turn whole-heartedly
to the Lord my God.

God watched over me
before I got to know him
and before I was wise
or distinguished good from evil.
He protected me and comforted me
as a father would his son.

I am unable to open my heart and mind
to those who are used to concise writing
in a way that my words
might express what I feel.
[But] I cannot be silent, nor should I,
about the great benefits of grace
which the Lord saw fit to confer on me
in the land of my captivity.

REPAYING GOD

The way [to] repay God
for correcting and taking notice of us
[is to] honour and praise his wonders
before every nation under heaven.

We… are… in the words of scripture,
a letter of Christ
bearing salvation
to the uttermost parts of the earth.

The letter may not be elegant
but it is assuredly and most powerfully
written on your hearts,
not with ink
but with the spirit of the living God.

THE SPIRIT

The Spirit is a witness
that even rustic ways
have been created
by the Most High.

I am …
an untaught refugee …
who does not know how to provide
for the future.

LIFTED UP

I was like a stone
lying in the deep mud …
Then he who is mighty came
and in his mercy
he not only pulled me out
but lifted me up
and placed me
at the very top of the wall.

I must, therefore, speak publicly
in order to repay the Lord
for such wonderful gifts ...
gifts for the present and for eternity
which the human mind cannot measure.

Let you be astonished,
you great and small
who revere God!

God inspired me with fear,
reverence and patience
to be the one who would if possible
serve the people faithfully
to whom the love of Christ brought me.

The love of Christ
gave me to the Irish
to serve them humbly and sincerely
for my entire lifetime
if I am found worthy.

The Irish

I must fearlessly and confidently
spread the name of God everywhere
in order to leave a legacy after my death
to my brothers and children,
the many thousands of them,
whom I have baptised in the Lord.

IRELAND

I am not at all worthy
to receive so many graces …
The Lord gave much to me,
his little servant,
more than as a young man
I ever hoped for or even considered.

When I had come to Ireland
I was tending herds every day
and I used to pray
many times during the day.
More and more
the love of God and reverence for him
came to me.

PRAYER

My faith increased
and the spirit was stirred up
so that in the course of a single day
I would say as many as a hundred prayers,
and almost as many in the night.

PRAYER

I prayed
even when I was staying in the woods
and on the mountain.
Before dawn I used to be roused up
to pray in snow or frost or rain.
I never felt the worse for my prayers …
I now realise,
the Spirit was burning within me.

In my sleep one night
I heard a voice saying:
' … soon you will go to your own country
… Look, your ship is ready …'
I ran away and left the man
with whom I had spent six years …
The power of God directed my way
and nothing daunted me
until I reached the ship.

ESCAPE

I spoke to the crew …
but the captain retorted:
'On no account are you to go with us.' …
I began to pray, and before I had ended
I heard loud shouting:
'Come quickly …'
I went back … and they began to say to me:
'Come on, we will take you on trust' …
and we set sail at once.

After three days we came to land
and for twenty-eight days
we made our way through deserted country.
Supplies ran out
and the party was worse for hunger.
The captain said to me:
'… You say your God is great
and all powerful;
why then can you not pray for us?'

ESCAPE

I said confidently:
'Turn sincerely with your whole heart
to the Lord my God
because nothing is impossible for him,
that this day he may send you food …
until you are satisfied;
for he has plenty everywhere.'

ESCAPE

With the help of God a herd of pigs
suddenly appeared on the road ...;
they killed many
and stopped there for two nights ...
After this
they gave profuse thanks to God
and I became honourable in their eyes.

Elijah

That night when I was asleep
Satan tempted me with a violence
which I will remember
as long as I am in this body …
How did it occur to me in my ignorance
to call on Elijah?

ELIJAH

While I was shouting 'Elijah! Elijah!' …
the brilliance of the sun
fell suddenly on me
and lifted my depression at once.
I believe that I was sustained
by Christ my Lord and that his Spirit
was even then calling out on my behalf.

CAPTIVE AGAIN

After many years
I was taken captive again …
On the sixtieth night the Lord rescued me
from my captors' hands.
A few years later,
I was in Britain with my relatives
who begged that I never leave them
in view of the hardships I had endured …

THE VOICE OF THE IRISH

One night I saw the vision
of a man called Victor,
who appeared to have come from Ireland
with an unlimited number of letters.
He gave me one
and I read the opening words:
'The voice of the Irish.'

The voice of the Irish

At the same moment
I seemed to hear the voice of those …
near the Western Sea.
They shouted with one voice:
'We ask you, holy boy,
come and walk once more among us.'

I was cut to the heart
and could read no more
and so I learned by experience …
After very many years
the Lord answered their cry.

THE VOICE OF GOD

Another night …
I heard … the following statement
at the end of prayer:
'He who gave his life for you,
he it is who is speaking in you.'
At that I awoke full of joy.

On another occasion
I saw a person praying within me.
I was as it seemed inside my body
and I heard him over me,
that is, over the inner man.
He was praying with great emotion.

I wondered greatly
who could possibly be praying inside me.
He spoke, at the end of the prayer,
saying that he was the Spirit …
I learned by experience
and I recalled the words of the apostle:
The Lord our Advocate pleads for us.

TRIAL

I was put on trial
by a number of my seniors
who cast up my sins
as unfitting for my laborious episcopate.
That day indeed
the impulse was overpowering to fall away
not only here and now, but forever.

TRIAL

But the Lord graciously spared
his exile and wanderer
and helped me greatly
when I was walked on in this way …
I pray God
that it may not be accounted to them
as a sin.

TRIAL

The charge against me
which they discovered after thirty years,
was a confession… to my dearest friend
[about] what I had done in my boyhood
one day, in one hour indeed,
because I had not yet overcome
my sinful ways.

TO IRELAND

I went to Ireland only with reluctance…
purified by the Lord.
He improved me so much
from my former condition
that I now care and work
for the salvation of others
whereas then
I did not even consider my own.

Thanks be to God
who supported me in everything …
I say boldly that my conscience
does not reproach me …
God is my witness
that I have told no lies
in my account to you.

LIES

I know well
the statement of the Lord
in the psalm:
A lying mouth
destroys the soul.

GOD

I cannot hide the gift of God
which he gave me
in the land of my captivity.
I sought him vigorously then
and there I found him.
I am convinced that God kept me
from all evil because of his Spirit
who lives in me …

GOD

I give thanks to my God tirelessly
who kept me faithful in the day of trial.
Who am I, Lord, and what is my calling
that you should co-operate with me
with such divine power?

GOD

I offer sacrifice to God confidently,
the living sacrifice of my life
to Christ, my Lord,
who preserved me in all my troubles.

GOD

I praise and proclaim God's name
in all places,
not only when things go well
but also in times of stress.

GOD

Whether I receive good or ill,
I return thanks equally to God,
who taught me always to trust him
unreservedly.

GOD

God's answer to my prayer inspired me …
to undertake
this holy and wonderful work
in spite of my ignorance,
and to imitate those who …
preach the Good News …
to all nations
before the end of the world.

GOOD NEWS

We are witnesses
that the Good News has been preached
in distant parts,
in places beyond which nobody lives.

GOOD NEWS

I came to the Irish heathens
to preach the Good News
and to put up with insults
from unbelievers…
I gave up my free-born status
for the good of others.

IN IRELAND I WISH TO DIE

Should I be worthy
I am ready to give my life
for his name's sake;
and it is in Ireland that I wish to spend it
until I die,
if the Lord should grant it to me.

BORN AGAIN

I am very much in debt to God,
who gave me so much grace
that through me
many people should be born again
in God.

We ought to fish well and diligently
in accordance with the advic
and teaching of the Lord, who says:
Follow me,
and I will make you fishers of men.

How does it happen in Ireland
that a people who
in their ignorance of God
worshipped idols
have lately become a people of the Lord
and are called children of God?

How is it
that the sons and daughters
of Scoto-Irish chieftains
are seen to be monks and virgins
dedicated to Christ?

The virgins… often suffer persecution
and unfair abuse…
The women who live in slavery
suffer the most.
They have to endure terror and threats
all the time.
But the Lord has given grace to many
and they follow him steadfastly.

What if I should consider leaving them
and going to Britain?
How dearly would I love to go,
like a man going to his homeland
and relatives …
God knows how much I yearned for it,
but I am tied by the Spirit.

I am afraid of undoing the work
which I have begun.
It was ... the Lord who commanded me
to come [to Ireland] and stay ...
for the rest of my life.
The Lord ... will protect me.

I do not trust myself
as long as I am in this mortal body.
Strong is the enemy who tries every day
to turn me away from
the faith and purity of that true religion
to which I have devoted myself
to the end of my life
for Christ my Lord.

I have not altogether
led a life as perfect as other believers …
I confess it to my Lord
and I do not blush in his sight
because I am not telling lies.

From my early manhood
when I came to know him,
the love of God and reverence for him
has grown in me,
and up to now,
by the favour of God,
I have kept the faith.

Keeping the Faith

I must return unending thanks to God
who often pardoned my folly
and my carelessness,
and on more than one occasion
spared me his great wrath …
I failed to realise in good time
the grace that was in me.
It is obvious to me now
what I should have understood earlier.

Believe me because of what I foretold
and still foretell in order
to strengthen and consolidate your faith.
Would that you, too, would reach out
to greater things and do better!
This will be my happiness,
because *a wise son is the glory of his father.*

You know, as does God,
how I have behaved among you
from my early manhood,
with genuine faith
and a sincere heart.

God knows I have cheated none …
nor would the thought occur to me,
lest I should provoke persecutions …
or that through me
the name of the Lord
would be blasphemed.

INTEGRITY

Mine was the long-term view
and for that reason
I used to take every precaution
so that the heathens
might not catch me out on any grounds
of infidelity concerning myself
or the work of my ministry.

INTEGRITY

I was unwilling to give unbelievers
even the slightest opportunity
for slander or disparagement.

INTEGRITY

Until we meet God …
I am spending,
and will go on spending more.
The Lord has power to allow me
ultimately to spend myself
in the interest of your souls.

INTEGRITY

Sufficient is the esteem
that is not yet seen
but that is felt in the heart.

HUMILITY

In the world
I have been exalted beyond measure
by the Lord ...
I was neither worthy of this
nor a likely choice for the privilege.

HUMILITY

Even if I wished for it
I have no wealth,
nor do I pass judgement on myself
in this matter.

TRUST IN GOD

I daily expect to be murdered or robbed
or reduced to slavery
in one way or another.
Not that I fear any of these things.

Because of his promises
I leave myself
in the hands of almighty God
who rules everywhere.

TRUST IN GOD

I entrust my soul to God,
who is most faithful
and for whom I am an ambassador
in my humble station.

No favourites

God has no favourites.

What return can I make to God
for all his goodness to me?
What can I say or what can I promise
to my Lord since any ability I have
comes from him?
Suffice it for God
to look into my heart and mind.

My only prayer to God
is that it may never happen
that I should lose his people
which he won for himself
at the end of the earth.

I ask God for perseverance,
to grant that I remain
a faithful witness to him
for his own sake
until my passing from this life.

Though I should be denied a grave,
though my corpse should be
utterly torn to pieces
and scattered to dogs and wild animals,
though the birds of the air
should devour it,
I would be fully confident …
that I have saved both body and soul.

We will undoubtedly rise
in the brightness of the sun,
that is, in the glory
of Christ Jesus our Redeemer,
as sons of the living God,
joint heirs with Christ
and made in his image.

The sun which we see rises daily
at his command for our benefit,
but will never reign,
nor its brilliance endure.
We believe in and worship Christ
the true sun who will never perish,
nor will anyone who does his will.

[The faithful] will remain for ever
as Christ remains for ever,
who reigns with God the Father Almighty
and the Holy Spirit before time began
and now and for all eternity.
Amen.

A request of those
who believe and revere God.
If any of you see fit
to examine this document,
which has been written
in Ireland by Patrick,
do not attribute to me the little I achieved.
Let your conclusion be the real truth,
that my success was the gift of God.

The Writings of St Patrick

Letter to
the Soldiers of Coroticus

I, Patrick, a sinner and untaught,
established in Ireland,
declare myself to be a bishop …
With my own hand
I have written down these words.
I composed them to be related
and passed on,
in order that they may be sent
to the soldiers of Coroticus.

In their hostile behaviour
they live in death ...
Dripping with blood
they wallow in
the slaughter of innocent Christians,
whom I personally brought
into the life of the baptised
and confirmed in Christ.

The newly-baptised
in their white garments
had just been anointed with chrism.
It was still giving forth its scent
on their foreheads
when they were
cruelly and brutally murdered,
put to the sword by these men …

PERSECUTION

The enemy shows his jealousy
through the tyranny of Coroticus,
a man without respect
either for God
or for his priests whom he chose …
that those whom they bind on earth
should be bound also in heaven.

PERSECUTION

I do not know
for whom I am to grieve the more;
whether for those who were killed,
for those whom they captured,
or those whom the devil
has deeply ensnared …
As scripture says:
Lord, the wicked have destroyed your law …

PERSECUTION

… your law which but recently
he had in his kindness
successfully planted in Ireland,
and which was taught by God's favour.

Repent

I make these special requests of you …
You must first make reparation to God
through rigorous penance
and in floods of tears.
You must free the servants of God
and baptised handmaids of Christ,
for whom he died and was crucified.

REPENT

The Most High rejects
the gifts of the wicked.

Offering sacrifice
from the property of the poor
is just as evil as slaughtering a son
in the presence of his father.
The riches, says scripture,
which he gathered unjustly
shall be vomited up from his belly …
unquenchable fire shall devour him.

Repentance

Avarice is a deadly sin.

You shall not covet your neighbour's goods.

You shall not kill.

MURDER

A murderer cannot be with Christ.

MURDER

He who hates his brother
is to be considered a murderer.
He who does not love his brother
remains in death.

GOD'S WILL

It was not without reference to God
or for merely human purposes
that I came to Ireland.

GOD'S WILL

It is not my virtue but God
who put this concern into my heart
that I should become one of the huntsmen
or fishermen
whom God once foretold
would come in the last days.

PLUNDER

I am looked on with hate.
What am I to do, Lord?
I am gretly despised.
Look, your sheep
are torn to pieces around me
and plundered
by that miserable band of robbers
at the bidding of the evil-minded
Coroticus.

PLUNDER

Ravenous wolves have gobbled up
the flock of the Lord,
which in Ireland under excellent care
was really flourishing,
countless sons of Scoto-Irish
and the daughters of their kings
having become monks and virgins
for Christ.

PLUNDER

Just as Eve did not understand
that it was death
she was offering her husband ...
so are all who do evil:
by causing death
they bring about
their eternal punishment.

The wickedness of the wicked
has prevailed over us.
We have been treated like aliens.
Perhaps they do not believe … that we
have one and the same God as Father.
They think it a matter of contempt
that we are Irish.
Scripture says: *Have you not one God?*
Why have you abandoned each one of you
his neighbour?

GOD'S GLORY

I lament for you, my dearly beloved.
But again, I rejoice in my heart.
I have not laboured for nothing …
I can see you:
You have begun to journey
where night will be no more,
nor mourning nor death …

You will reign
with apostles and prophets and martyrs.
You will receive everlasting kingdoms …
Outside shall be
the dogs and sorcerers and murderers …

EARTH'S TRANSIENCE

As for Coroticus and his criminals,
  rebels against Christ,
    where will they see themselves,
      men who distribute
        young baptised woman as spoil
in the service of a vile earthly kingdom
  which may disappear in a moment?

EARTH'S TRANSIENCE

Like a cloud of smoke
dispersed by the wind,
deceitful sinners will perish
when God approaches.

I request the servant of God
who will readily be
the bearer of this letter,
that on no account should it be withdrawn
… but should be read
before all the communities
and even in the presence
of Coroticus himself.

If God inspires [the soldiers of Coroticus]
that at some time or other
they may come to their senses again
in his regard, that they may repent,
even at the last minute,
of their wicked crime …
may they have peace in the Father,
and in the Son, and in the Holy Spirit.
Amen.

My decision to write must be made
in the light of our faith in the Trinity.
The gift of God
and his eternal consolation
must be made known,
regardless of danger.

God in the Trinity

THE HOLY TRINITY

There is no other God,
there never was
and there never will be,
than God the Father …

The holy trinity

… unbegotten and without beginning,
from whom is all beginning
holding all things as we have learned;

The holy trinity

… and his son Jesus Christ
whom we declare
to have been always with the Father
and to have been begotten
spiritually by the Father …

... in a way which baffles description,
before the beginning of the world,
before all beginning;
and through him are made
all things,
visible and invisible ...

The holy trinity

We believe in him
and we look for his coming soon
as judge of the living and of the dead,
who will treat every person
according to their deeds.

THE HOLY TRINITY

God has poured out
the Holy Spirit
on us
in abundance …

He has poured
on us the gift
and guarantee
of eternal life ...